Learning to Fall

RECORDING THE BLESSINGS OF AN IMPERFECT LIFE

By Philip Simmons

Peter Pauper Press, Inc.
White Plains, New York

For Kathryn, Amelia, and Aaron

The text in this book is excerpted from Learning to Fall:
The Blessings of an Imperfect Life, *by Philip Simmons,*
published by Bantam Books, a division of Random House, Inc.
Copyright © 2000 by Philip Simmons.
All rights reserved.

Designed by Helana Shull

Visit us at www.peterpauper.com

CONTENTS

Dear Friends,

The journal you hold in your hands invites you to reflect upon the personal and spiritual issues we all must face during our lives. By learning to fall, I mean learning to live richly in the face of the losses we inevitably suffer as human beings. Since being diagnosed with Lou Gehrig's disease nine years ago, I've certainly suffered my share of losses, but I've also been given an extraordinary chance to practice consciously the art of living and dying. Some of the fruits of that practice are offered here in the form of passages and questions that prompt you to explore, as I have, the harrowing business of rescuing joy from heartbreak.

My wife, Kathryn, was here a moment ago, reading over this letter. "Tell them," she said, "that if you hadn't given yourself the time to write and reflect, you wouldn't be alive right now." And I guess she's right. At least for now, writing has saved my life. In many ways, I count myself lucky. I spend my days in a wheelchair, I can't lift my arms, I can't hike in the woods or hug my children, I can't wash dishes or fold laundry. Life's pleasures, and also its ordinary labors, are being taken from me. But I'm being shown what's essential: that we must continue to do whatever remains within our power. I can still help my kids with their homework, I can enjoy a good dinner with friends, and I can watch the bull moose that walked across our frosted field this morning, blowing clouds of steam. And as long as I'm able, I'll keep writing, keep saving my life, one word at a time.

Wherever in your journey my words find you, may they help you on your way.

Wishing you every blessing,

Philip Simmons
Sandwich, New Hampshire
December, 2001

MYSTERY

AT ITS DEEPEST LEVELS LIFE IS NOT A PROBLEM, but a mystery. The distinction is fundamental: problems are to be solved, true mysteries are not. At one time or another, each of us confronts an experience so powerful, bewildering, joyous, or terrifying that all our efforts to see it as a "problem" are futile. Each of us is brought to the cliff's edge. At such moments we can either back away in bitterness or confusion, or leap forward into mystery . . .

Where in your life have you experienced mystery?

WHEN WE STOP SEEING THE WORLD as a "problem" to be solved, when instead we open our hearts to the mystery of our common suffering, we may find ourselves where we least expected to be: in a world transformed by love.

How do you respond to problems in your life?

What usually happens in your mind when you fail to solve a problem?

What problems in your life are you ready to give up trying to solve?

THERE'S A WELL-KNOWN ZEN PARABLE about the man who was crossing a field when he saw a tiger charging at him. The man ran, but the tiger gained on him, chasing him toward the edge of a cliff. When he reached the edge, the man had no choice but to leap. He had one chance to save himself: a scrubby branch growing out of the side of the cliff about half way down. He grabbed the branch and hung on. Looking down, what did he see on the ground below? Another tiger.

Then the man saw that a few feet off to his left a small plant grew out of the cliff, and from it there hung one ripe strawberry. Letting go with one hand he found that he could stretch his arm out just far enough to pluck the berry with his fingertips and bring it to his lips.

How sweet it tasted!

We're used to getting nuggets of conventional advice:

- Don't wait for a tragedy to start appreciating the little things in life.
- Stop and smell the honeysuckle.
- Count your blessings. Appreciate what you have instead of complaining about what you don't.

But I prefer to offer these mystery points:

? If spiritual growth is what you seek, don't ask for more strawberries, ask for more tigers.
? The threat of the tigers, the leap from the cliff, are what give the strawberry its savor. . . . No tigers, no sweetness.
? In falling we somehow gain what means most. In falling we are given back our lives even as we lose them.

What does it mean, for you, to live with mystery?

_____

_____

_____

_____

_____

_____

_____

_____

_____

_____

_____

_____

WE ARE ALL—ALL OF US—FALLING. We are all, now, this moment, in the midst of that descent, fallen from heights that may now seem only a dimly remembered dream, falling toward a depth we can only imagine, glimpsed beneath the water's surface shimmer. And so let us pray that if we are falling from grace, let us also fall *with* grace, *to* grace. If we are falling toward pain and weakness, let us also fall toward sweetness and strength. If we are falling toward death, let us also fall toward life.

ACCEPTANCE

AT SOME POINT we all confront the fact that each of us, each individual soul is, as the poet William Butler Yeats says, "fastened to a dying animal." We're all engaged in the business of dying, whether consciously or not, slowly or not. For me, knowing that my days are numbered has meant the chance to ask with new urgency the sorts of questions most of us avoid: everything from "What is my life's true purpose?" to "Should I reorganize my closets?"

Lately I've come to feel quite strongly that answering these questions begins with acceptance. Not resignation, not passivity, but a profound and thorough acceptance of our place in the natural order. Not only must we accept our own deaths as a necessary part of that order, but we must come to see that it is our very mortality that calls us to act according to our highest nature. It is out of our acceptance of all that we are, including and especially that we are creatures that will one day die, that we are called to our highest human duties. Death, in other words, is good for us.

In accepting death, what in life becomes most important to you?
How can this acceptance guide your everyday life?

WE USUALLY DEAL WITH LOSS by reminding ourselves of what we still have. The approach I've found more helpful is also more difficult. It is born out of a paradox: that we deal most fruitfully with loss by accepting the fact that we will one day lose everything. When we learn to fall, we learn that only by letting go our grip on all that we ordinarily find most precious—our achievements, our plans, our loved ones, our very selves—can we find, ultimately, the most profound freedom. In the act of letting go of our lives, we return more fully to them.

What would it feel like to accept your own death thoroughly?

AS I SEE IT, we know we're truly grown up when we stop trying to fix people. About all we can really do for people is to love them and treat them with kindness. That goes for ourselves, too. That goes for ourselves *especially*. I've given up on self-improvement. (I've also decided I no longer have to floss.)

How have you tried to change the people in your life?

How does it feel to accept them as they are?

I ONCE STOPPED MY CAR in the middle of a bridge to let a turtle cross. It must have climbed out of the stream some fifteen feet below, and I got out of my car to watch it haul itself across the asphalt until it reached the bridge's edge, and then, not knowing it was on a bridge, tip over the edge to plunge back down into the stream from which it had come. Though I don't know how the turtle felt about this, I felt awful. But while I was busy entertaining my frustration at the wasted effort, while I was busy making the turtle's fall an emblem for all the botched beginnings and abrupt endings of my days, the turtle was busy swimming to the shore and hauling itself out to begin the long climb up the bank again. As if to say to me, where I stood swaddled in my mooning and moaning self, as if to say, "See? See how I dance? See how it's done?"

What does acceptance feel like? How does it differ from resignation or passivity?

What blessings can you find among the hurdles life has placed in your path?

I TOOK AN IMMEDIATE LIKING TO [the Roman emperor Marcus] Aurelius. He slept on a bare board, ate little, prayed to his gods, and commanded an empire. He thought continually of his own death, and when I read his words I knew I had met a soul worth reckoning with:

> *Let it make no difference to thee whether thou art cold or warm, if thou art doing thy duty; and whether thou art drowsy or satisfied with sleep; and whether ill-spoken or praised; and whether dying or doing something else. For it is one of the acts of life, this act by which we die: it is sufficient then in this act also to do well what we have in hand.*

Whether dying *or doing something else*. The casualness of that phrase! I imagine Aurelius getting off of his board in the morning and making his to-do list for the day:

1. Breakfast with Faustina
2. Address the Senate on the need to defend the northern frontier
3. Prune rose bushes, sacrifice goat
4. Die?
5. If not, lead army against the barbarians

When times are hard, what gets you up in the morning?

Do not despise death, but be well content with it, since this too is one of those things which nature wills. . . . As thou waitest for the time when the child shall fall out of thy wife's womb, so be ready for the time when thy soul shall fall out of this envelope.

To accept death is to live with a profound sense of freedom. The freedom, first, from attachment to the things of this life that don't really matter: fame, material possessions, and even, finally, our own bodies. Acceptance brings the freedom to live fully in the present. The freedom, finally, to act according to our highest nature:

Everywhere and at all times it is in thy power piously to acquiesce in thy present condition, and to behave justly to those about thee.

Only when we accept our present condition can we set aside fear and discover the love and compassion that are our highest human endowments. And out of our compassion we deal justly with those about us. Not just on our good days, not just when it's convenient, but *everywhere and at all times* we are free to act according to that which is highest in us. And in such action we find peace.

Record for a week at least one moment each day when you act "according to what is highest in you," whether or not it's convenient.

Day 1

Day 2

Day 3

Day 4

Day 5

Day 6

_____

_____

_____

_____

_____

_____

_____

_____

_____

_____

_____

_____

EACH DAY THAT I CAN GET OUT OF BED in the morning, I am blessed. Each day that any of us can move our limbs to do the world's work, we are blessed. And if limbs wither, and speech fails, we are still blessed. So long as this heart beats, I am blessed, for it is our human work, it is our human duty, finally, to rise each day in the face of loss, to rise in the face of grief, of debility, of pain, to move as the turtle moves, her empty nest behind her, her labor come to nothing, up out of the pit and toward the next season's doing.

IMPERFECTION

SPRING ENLIVENS US, yet from our human vantage not all resurrections are equally welcome. . . . If you don't live in the north woods, you won't understand what I mean by this. Vacationers who come for a week in August have little idea that the year-round folks have just survived plagues rivaling those visited on Pharaoh's Egypt. . . . All nature clamors for our blood, and who can blame it? Bugs seek nothing we don't seek for ourselves: to eat before being eaten, to be fruitful and multiply. But what designing genius fashioned the mosquito? Who decided that it needed seven mouth parts—no more, no less—to grip and drill and pump and suck? And who developed the tag team format whereby, just as the mosquitoes tire in July, the deer flies arrive to burrow through our sun-warmed hair and chew our scalps?

What in your life is imperfect?

WE HAVE ALL HEARD POEMS, SONGS, AND PRAYERS that exhort us to see God in a blade of grass, a drop of dew, a child's eyes, or the petals of a flower. But that's too easy. . . . Our greater challenge is to see God not only in the eyes of the suffering child but in the suffering itself. To thank God for broken bones and broken hearts, for everything that opens us to the mystery of our humanness. The challenge is to stand at the sink with your hands in the dishwater, fuming over a quarrel with your spouse, children at your back clamoring for attention, the radio blasting the latest bad news, and to say "God is here, now, in this room, here in this dishwater, in this dirty spoon."

Is it easier to recall life's perfect moments or its imperfections?
Are there more imperfect moments than perfect ones? Why?

DON'T TALK TO ME ABOUT FLOWERS and sunshine and waterfalls: this is the ground, here, now, in all that is ordinary and imperfect, this is the ground in which life sows the seeds of our fulfillment. The imperfect is our paradise.

Have your experiences of imperfection, loss, or suffering brought your life greater richness or depth? Have they brought you closer to what you might call God or Spirit? How?

As T. S. Eliot writes:

We shall not cease from exploration
And the end of all our exploring
Will be to arrive where we started
And know the place for the first time.

ON OUR BAD DAYS, in our dark moments, we see in our unfinished houses the surest sign of calamity. That unpainted drywall, that missing piece of trim remind us that the world is too much with us, that we have lost our grip, that life hurls more at us than we can handle. At such times we find ourselves aboard time's driverless train, rushing toward doom.

When you remember your unfinished tasks, both great and small, what feelings arise in you?

[IN] PAUL'S WORDS: "we know that if the earthly house we live in is destroyed, we have a building from God, a house not made with hands, eternal in the heavens." . . .

The unsettling news is that we'll never reach that elsewhere of our longing as long as we remain in this life. . . . When our fantasies of a better life consume us, when our memories of past hurts bind us and fears of pending calamity drive us, we are robbed of the only gift—the greatest gift—we can be sure of possessing: the present moment.

What kinds of things keep you from living more fully in the present moment?

IN EACH UNFINISHED AND IMPERFECT DAY I struggle to find myself at home in this body, however flawed and failing, in this breath, however labored, in this speech, however halting. Each day, I work to make my home among the people I find about me. I write these words to make a sort of house in which you and I may dwell together for a time. . . . We are here, in the unfinished house of the now, for the duration. The joy is in the building.

Can you recall a time in your life, whether a moment or a stretch of years, when you were able to live fully in the present moment? What does it take for you to be able to do that?

_____

_____

_____

_____

_____

_____

_____

_____

_____

_____

_____

_____

_____

_____

_____

[W]HAT WOULD IT MEAN TO EXPERIENCE OUR OWN ACTIONS in such a way that the terms "good" and "bad" don't apply? It would mean living, like animals, without doubt as to our life's purpose. It would mean living in such perfect alignment with that purpose that our every act flowed effortlessly from what was highest and truest within us. It would mean rising each day to forage or feed, to shelter and care for our young, to laze or labor, fight or frolic without distraction, without self-judgment, without taking one step off life's true path. And even in the face of misery and terror, even as we walk through the valley of the shadow of death, even as the sleet freezes our hides or the hawk descends upon us, it would mean living in the faith that this, too, is the way.

What would you say is your life's highest purpose?

WE DON'T GO INTO WILDNESS to escape our lives but to return to them, to return to our true selves and our highest purposes. . . . We practice wildness so that we may live more fully and constantly in the midst of *anima*, in the midst of soul. . . . Wildness will not save us from misfortune. Fear, doubt, grief all lie in wait to strike and seize us as before. Only now their grip will not be so tight or last so long. In life's thicket we will have created a clearing for our wild selves. And in that clearing, in the face of confusion and worry, in the face of failure and loss, in the face of death itself, we will lift our noses to the moon and sing.

When do you feel most connected to yourself—your highest, truest self?

[N]OTHING SERVES RELATIONSHIPS, families, or communities better than a well-cultivated solitude. Having given generously and fully to ourselves, we can give generously and fully to each another and our children and, by extension, to our communities.

In your life, how do you find the balance between being alone and being with others?

WE SEE OTHERS AS STRANGERS only when we are estranged from ourselves. We can fear in others only what we fear in ourselves. And when we meet a loved one, we are meeting ourselves as the beloved. . . . It's in those moments that we go out of ourselves, and simultaneously go into ourselves, into our own essential goodness. At such moments we surrender all advantages, give up all claims to righteousness, relinquish all privileges except that of being in the presence—the sacred and unfathomable presence—of another.

Write about a time when you felt deeply connected to both yourself and others.

I'VE LEARNED that, as much as we seek to avoid the mud in our lives, we need the mud for what grows from it. Every mud season is a kind of death, with resurrection lying on the other side. In the mud painting my daughter did at school, the great brown swath across the bottom two-thirds of the paper is topped with tiny, bright flowers. The image suggests causality—mud makes flowers—but also necessity: no mud, no flowers. As I enter my various mud seasons, I've learned to ask: what death is this? Or what is it within me that needs to die? And out of this death, what resurrection will come?

What hopes, ideals, abilities, or people have you had to let go of?

_____

_____

_____

_____

_____

_____

_____

_____

_____

_____

_____

_____

_____

_____

_____

What is your usual response to the "muddy" parts of life—to mishap, misfortune, or disappointment? Have you ever found that going through a "mud season" changed you somehow for the good?

THE EXAMPLE OF JESUS, and the experience of mud season, remind me of a harsh truth: to be reborn, we first must die. The way to Jerusalem lies through mud. Dying, like mud, can take many forms, but every death, in the sense I mean, is a letting go. We let go of ambition, of pride, of ego. We let go of relationships, of perfect health, of loved ones who go before us to their own deaths. We let go of insisting that the world be a certain way. Letting go of any of these things can seem the failure of every design, the loss of every cherished hope. But in letting them go, we may also let go fear, let go our white-knuckled grip on a life that never seems to meet our expectations, let go our anguished hold on smaller selves our spirits have outgrown.

Have you ever experienced a "resurrection"? What had to die in order for the resurrection to take place?

I IMAGINE JESUS THE MAN AS ONE OF GOD'S MANY EMBODIMENTS in the world, and I imagine Jesus the Christ as that potential divinity within each of us. When we enter into that which is divine within us, we enter our own Christhood, our own Christ-consciousness. To stand fully within that presence, to live and move in such alignment with the divine and natural order that the very stones would shout out our arrival, is to enter our highest, anointed selves. And what New Testament tradition describes as Jesus' resurrection and return to the Father represents for us the possibility of a return to God by whatever name we choose to call it: the Higher Self, Brahman, the ground of Being.

What possibilities for resurrection do you see in your life now? What might that new life be like?

_____

_____

_____

_____

_____

_____

_____

_____

_____

_____

_____

THIS IS HEADY STUFF, I know. For most of us a mystical experience consists of finding a parking space with time left on the meter. For much of my life I've lived contentedly by a few simple rules: don't track mud in the house, take care of your own, help others, do as little harm as you can, change your oil every 3,000 miles. But maybe enlightenment is simpler than we think.

I've been told that religion boils down to two beliefs: first, that there is something of ultimate significance in the universe; second, that there is a way of being connected to it. Each of the world's religions offers a distinct way of connecting, and each of us must find his or her own way in to ultimate significance. Prayer, meditation, and selfless service are all honored methods. The Buddhist monk Thich Nhat Hanh has taught me that, if done right, washing dishes can serve as well.

How do you connect to "ultimate significance"?

_____

_____

_____

_____

_____

_____

_____

_____

_____

_____

_____

HARRIED, OVERWORKED, AND OVERWHELMED AS WE ARE, we often experience our students, patients, clients, colleagues, and children as difficult, irresponsible, rude, dull, or simply too numerous to keep track of. But if we mean to choose the world, we must see God in the people who come under our care. That is, we must see them as at bottom no different from ourselves. No matter our busyness, no matter our own or others' flaws, we need at some point to see every human being as a marvel, a berry held up in sunlight, worthy of wonder.

Think about the people around you: family, friends, colleagues, acquaintances.
In what ways are all these people no different from you?

I SOMETIMES IMAGINE that if the creator of the universe wanted to take another shot at communicating what was most important, she might replace all of sacred scripture with the words "Pay Attention!" To choose the world means first of all to see it clearly, to shed fantasy and habit, to look, and look again, to let ourselves be broken open by its intricacy and its mystery.

Write down each day for a week your observations gleaned from looking at the world in a new and different way.

Day 1

Day 2

Day 3

Day 4

Day 5

Day 6

Day 7

SCIENTIFIC SEEING, FOR GOOD REASONS, SEEKS TO FIX the world like a bug pinned to a tray, wants to make it fully *present* to our rational understanding. Mystical seeing, on the other hand, discovers both presence and absence equally.

When I hold the berry in my hand, when I surrender myself wholly to its presence, I know I'm in the presence of the Divine. But at the same time, I come to know the berry as a mystery beyond my comprehension, and I come to know God as that which is essentially unknowable. Mystical seeing always involves this paradox, and thus can be as harrowing as it is uplifting.

To approach God is to know the infinite distance between God and us; to know God is to enter what one medieval mystic called "the cloud of unknowing." Each moment of light and clarity brings darkness and confusion. I possess all knowledge, all wisdom, all joy, and at the same moment I'm empty and cast down, groveling with Job before the voice out of the whirlwind. . . .

WE MUST SEE THE WORLD as scientists, but first as lovers. . . . We must love the world with a child's love for its parents, a love immediate and unreserved, no matter that the world gives us both blueberries and the black flies that torment us as we pick them. . . . We must love the world as new lovers do one another, as if to be in the beloved's presence is to walk through a world made newly luminous, finding that every ordinary gesture . . . is holy and part of a sacred dance. Mystic vision is a lover's vision, and despite the pain love brings, to see the world through a lover's eyes is already to have chosen it.

Is there a way for you to balance "scientific" and "mystic" vision in your life?

. . . *The Cloud of Unknowing* tells us that "all rational beings possess two faculties, the power of knowing and the power of loving. To the first, to the intellect, God who made them is forever unknowable, but to the second, to love, he is completely knowable, and that by every separate individual."

Our first act upon entering the world is to draw breath, to take some of its substance into ourselves. And with our first exhalation we give something of ourselves back to the world. The world moves through us as we move through the world, each breath a response, a renewal of that original promise. To choose the world is to return to where we began, to follow love to its source, to rest in that ground of our being that has no beginning and no ending.

EMPTINESS AND SILENCE

JUST AS SILENCE IS THE NECESSARY CONDITION or ground of speech, Buddhist "emptiness" is not negation but pure possibility, the condition or ground of being. In a cartoon I saw once, it's the Dalai Lama's birthday, and he's opening a gift-wrapped box, which turns out to be empty. Looking into it, the Dalai Lama says: "Nothing. Just what I've always wanted!"

You can think of my words here as offering the gift of an empty box, but you shouldn't think of me as having offered it. I merely point out that the gift has already been offered, is offered to you at every moment, is in fact all around you and within you, available as breath. All that remains is for you to accept it.

How might you reduce the noise in your life, both external noise and the "noise" inside your head?

EMPTINESS, LIKE SILENCE, LIKE LOVE, IS NOT SOMETHING WE CHOOSE, not something we reason our way into, but rather something into which we fall, something in which we *find ourselves*. The fall into emptiness, into silence, has the nature of an accident. And though we can't choose our accidents, we can learn to make ourselves accident prone. . . .

There are many ways to do this: you can meditate, attend religious services, practice Chopin études. What matters is that you find some way to point your sled downhill. You don't know where you'll land, but you must be willing to take the ride.

What can you do to make yourself more "accident prone"?

IN TOUCHING EMPTINESS we touch the source, the spring, the creative power out of which the universe flows at every moment. That source has many names, but I call it "God."

When are you most aware of what you would call the "sacred" or "God" or "the source of life"?

A WISE INDIAN YOGI ONCE SAID, "Before speaking, consider whether it is an improvement upon silence."

IN THE MIDST OF OUR WORKING AND DOING WE TAKE OUR STAND, we open ourselves to emptiness, as John Tarrant writes, "bringing the great background near, so that whatever we do, rising in the quiet, has force and beauty." Coming out of silence each word gains substance; coming out of emptiness each action grows distinct. . . . . [I]n taking our stand, we find ourselves free to speak in kindness and act for the good.

Whatever our personal circumstances, we can resist our fate and continue to suffer, or we can open ourselves to the fall into emptiness. We can choose to point our sleds downhill. The dark woods are waiting, but also the moon.

I THINK IF WE'RE HONEST WITH OURSELVES, we can agree that our busyness—whether of body or of mind—is often a distraction, a way of avoiding others, avoiding intimacy, avoiding ourselves. . . . These days, the idea of original sin has grown unfashionable, but to me it seems as good a way as any of naming that deep feeling of unworthiness so many of us suffer, driving us to hurl a lifetime of work and worry into a pit that can never be filled. Unchecked, this impulse can drag us into bitterness, loneliness, depression, and despair.

How easy is it for you to feel satisfied with your accomplishments?

How much do you worry about unfinished tasks?

AMERICANS IN GENERAL CANNOT REST from doing and acquiring, as though some winter of the spirit, if not of climate, were always just around the corner.

When was the last time you felt "all caught up" with the various tasks in your life? How long did it last? How did it feel, while it lasted?

WE WORK IN THE HOPEFUL if deluded belief that we can control our fates, in this world or the next. Our work denies our doom.

Is keeping busy ever a form of procrastination for you? A way of avoiding something?

WHAT IS IT, THEN, THAT RESTORES US to a better version of ourselves, that returns us to our firm sense of goodness—both our own and the world's? Perhaps it's a question of grace: a reflected sunset flares in the windows of a skyscraper, a sheet of newspaper takes flight down an empty street, and suddenly we find ourselves in a world made luminous with wonder. . . . And so it is: the world itself can call us out of our preoccupations, our worries, our lists and agendas. In such moments our attention is arrested, quite literally stopped, and the world seems to say to us: "Don't just do something, stand there."

When you feel "too busy" or "overwhelmed," what restores a sense of balance in your life?

IN THE MIDST OF A BUSY MORNING, with a long list of unfinished tasks, your daughter or granddaughter asks you to bake cookies and you surprise yourself by saying yes, so that for one hour the world stops and you give yourself the gift of being fully present to her small hands, to the pleasure of her company, to sweet sticky dough.

Is it hard for you to slow down or sit still? What happens when you do?

ON SOME LEVEL WE ARE ALWAYS SEARCHING for our life's work, wanting to align our doing and our being with our highest purposes. [In] moments of calm we find, to our surprise, that our life's work is here in our hands, at this very moment; it is here as we gaze into another's eyes, it is here in each breath we receive from and give back to the world.

What allows you to be fully absorbed in a task, without thinking about past or future?

. . . As the Tao says, "The world is ruled by letting things take their course."

AURELIUS WROTE: "Look within. Within is the fountain of good. And it will ever bubble up, if thou wilt ever dig." Finding this fountain of goodness within us, we discover that no land is foreign; no matter where we go, we are never strangers. We return home to the place we never left.

When life is off balance and out of control, how do you return to center?
What is your center?

WHAT WE'RE AFTER IS EQUANIMITY, the poise that allows us to accept gracefully the blessings and burdens that are beyond our control. What we're after is the ability, regardless of circumstance, in the face of disappointment and happy surprise, in the face of tragedy and bliss, to return home to our true selves and our highest natures.

How much of life is under your control? What are some things you can, and some things you cannot, control?

How do you respond to life's surprises? Write how you responded to a wonderful surprise, and to an unwelcome one.

IN OUR DAILY WORK, in our roles as caregivers and providers, in our manner of receiving the gifts and good works of others, we can be disciplined or not, mindful or not, responsible and responsive or not, but always our actions both shape and are shaped by the vessel of character. And traditionally, religious faith and spiritual practice are thought to strengthen this vessel, creating a sound container for our developing relationship to mystery, suffering, and the Divine.

Life throws things at us that we cannot predict and cannot control. What we can control is who we are along the way.

To what extent is your own character under your control?

_____

_____

_____

_____

_____

_____

_____

_____

_____

_____

_____

To what extent does character determine the way you respond to life's surprises?

ETERNAL LIFE

MORE AND MORE I FIND THAT DWELLING IN THE PRESENT MOMENT, in the face of everything that would call us out of it, is our highest spiritual discipline. More boldly, I would say that our very presentness is our salvation; the present moment, entered into fully, is our gateway to eternal life.

Now, when I say this, you could accuse me of being a mystic. . . . But mine is the mysticism of everyday life, of the heaped laundry and the bruised toe, of overcooked broccoli and leaves spangled with dew, of sunrise and sorrow, laughter and linguini, music and mold. This everyday mysticism requires no special powers, only imagination, a doting and practiced attention to the ordinary, a willingness to be surprised by grace.

Describe a "timeless" moment from your life, a moment where "time stood still" or where you felt as though you were living in eternity.

DWELLING IN THE MOMENT, on our breath, on the works of our hands immediately before us, we're drawn into life's luminousness, into the mystery at the heart of ordinary things. Dwelling in the present, at least at first, involves forgetting past and future, stopping the mind's whirlwind of memory and expectation, giving ourselves a blessed hour's calm as we meditate, bake bread, walk through the forest, or play games with a child.

But with further practice we may find past and future returning to our awareness, only now without bringing anxiety or distraction along with them. Instead, we become aware of living in eternity, knowing that this moment has found its proper place in the stream of all time. When we feel this way, the present moment enlarges, draws past and future into it, until we are dwelling not just in the moment but within the whole of life.

What in your life—or in your world, or in the universe—do you consider to be eternal and unchanging?

WHEN WE ACCEPT OUR IMPERMANENCE, letting go of our attachment to things as they are, we open ourselves to grace. When we can stand calmly in the face of our passing away, when we have the courage to look even into the face of a child and say, "This flower, too, will fade and be no more," when we can sense the nearness of death and feel its rightness equally with birth, then we will have crossed over to that farther shore where death can hold no fear for us, where we will know the measure of the eternal that is ours in this life.

Our journey takes us to suffering and sorrow, but there is a way through suffering to something like redemption, something like joy, to that larger version of ourselves that lives outside of time.

Some of us go willingly to the edge, some of us are driven to it, some of us find ourselves there by grace. But all of us get there at some time in our lives, when through the gateway of the present moment we glimpse something beyond. And when we do, may we open ourselves to wonder, may we surrender to the mystery that passes understanding, may we find ourselves at the threshold of this eternal life.

PHILIP SIMMONS is Associate Professor of English at Lake Forest College in Illinois, where he taught literature and creative writing for nine years before being disabled by Lou Gehrig's disease. He earned his B.A. in English and Physics from Amherst College, his M.F.A. in Creative Writing from Washington University in St. Louis, and his Ph.D. in English from the University of Michigan.

He lives in New Hampshire with his wife, artist Kathryn Field, and their children, Aaron and Amelia.

Visit Philip Simmons's website at www.learningtofall.com.

Photo courtesy of the Bantam Dell Publishing Group/Photo © Paul Simmons